THE BEST OF
WORDS
TO LIVE BY

D0834792

THE BEST OF
WORDS
TO LIVE BY

EDITED BY
WILLIAM NICHOLS

A POCKET BOOK SPECIAL
PUBLISHED BY POCKET BOOKS, INC.
IN ASSOCIATION WITH "THIS WEEK" MAGAZINE
NEW YORK
1966

ACKNOWLEDGMENTS

Permission has been granted to reprint the following material:
"On Motes and Beams" from *The Summing Up*, copyright 1938, by W. Somerset Maugham; by permission of Doubleday and Company, Inc.

"Peace of Mind" by Joshua Loth Liebman, from *Peace of Mind*, copyright 1946, by Joshua Loth Liebman; by permission of Simon and Schuster, Inc.

"Letter to a Little Girl" by F. Scott Fitzgerald, from *The Crack-Up* by F. Scott Fitzgerald. Copyright 1945 by New Directions. Reprinted by permission of New Directions, Publishers.

"On Love" by Erich Fromm, from *The Art of Loving*, copyright 1956 by Erich Fromm. By permission of Harper and Brothers.

"Oh, Those Days of Childhood" by Grandma Moses from *Grandma Moses, My Life's History*, edited by Otto Kallir and published by Harper and Brothers.

Copyright, ©, 1945, 1946, 1947, 1948, 1949 by William I. Nichols

Copyright, ©, 1947, 1948, 1949, 1950, 1951, 1952, 1953, 1954, 1955, 1956, 1957, 1958, 1959 by United Newspapers Magazine Corporation

Copyright, ©, 1955, 1956, 1957, 1958, 1959, 1960, 1961, 1962 by United Newspapers Magazine Corporation

Copyright, ©, 1966 by William I. Nichols

All rights reserved.

Published by Pocket Books, Inc., New York, and on the same day in Canada by Pocket Books of Canada, Ltd., Richmond Hill, Ontario.

Printed in the U.S.A.

"The way to do is to be."

—LAO-TSE

CONTENTS

ON SEEING THINGS CLEARLY

LIVING WITH THE WORLD

INTRODUCTION

This book is the flowering of an idea which began as an experiment, and then turned into rare adventure.

It started this way: Some time ago, I was reading a wise, quiet book by David Grayson called *Under My Elm,* in which this gentle philosopher told stories about rural life in his New England village with his country neighbors. It was a strangely restful book to read, especially in that year, 1945, when everybody was talking about the "end of our era," and the "doom of our civilization."

One chapter appealed to me especially. In it, Grayson described an old farmer-neighbor who was a kind of walking anthology. Whenever he ran across some bit of verse or prose he liked, this rural collector preserved it, slipped the words inside his hatband, to be tacked up later on his granary wall or the partitions of his horse barn.

"I thought afterward," Grayson wrote, "as I tramped up the town road, how most of us have collections of sayings we live by. . . . I believe it would be difficult to find an adult being who hasn't a saying or two, or more, that he is saving because it expresses something vital."

That chance paragraph from David Grayson's Amherst study set me to planning a fascinating voyage of discovery, not into barns and granaries, but into the minds and hearts of many people during a period when our world was seemingly plunged into doubt, pessimism, and fear.

The quest was to be an editorial venture, for I believed that words which had caught the imagination of one man or woman could be shared with others in the pages of *This Week* Magazine, where millions of men and women could make them part of their lives.

The first step was to select a list of people who, through their achievements, were what the world regards as successful. Then, to each of them went a letter which read like this: "These are times when millions of Americans are deeply disturbed and many of them are unhappy. We are surrounded by all comforts of a machine age, and yet we have somehow lost our sense of the meaning and purpose and beauty of life. Possibly you have faced the same problem. Perhaps you have found some words to live by, and treasured them because they say something which you regard as vital."

The appeal touched a rich source of inspiration. For years each issue of *This Week* opened with "words" which came in response to my letters, and which then flowed out to bring hope and comfort to others.

As the weeks went by, and the contributions kept coming in, I suddenly realized that here, in the truest sense, was philosophy in the making. One by one, the people of our time were bringing into me the wisdom gleaned from their own experience in living. Placed all together these fragments suddenly fell into a thrilling pattern, a rich mosaic—a way of life for our time.

WILLIAM NICHOLS

ON
LOVING
AND
LIKING

Liking Yourself

BY

JOHN STEINBECK

AUTHOR

"That which we are, we are . . . ."
—ALFRED, LORD TENNYSON

Once a friend of mine named Ed said to me, "For a very long time I didn't like myself." It was not said in self-pity but simply as an unfortunate fact. "It was a very difficult time," he said, "and very painful. I did not like myself for a number of reasons, some of them valid and some of them pure fancy. I would hate to have to go back to that.

"Then gradually," he said, "I discovered with surprise and pleasure that a number of people did like me. And I thought, If they can like me, why can't I like myself? Just thinking it did not do it, but slowly I learned to like myself and then it was all right."

This was not said in self-love in its bad connotation but in self-knowledge. He meant literally that he had learned to accept and like the person Ed as he liked other people. It gave him a great advantage. Most people do not like themselves at all. They distrust themselves, put on masks and pomposities. They quarrel and boast and pretend and are jealous because they do not like themselves. But mostly they do not even know themselves well enough to form a true liking, and since we automatically fear and dislike strangers, we fear and dislike our stranger-selves.

Once Ed was able to like himself he was released from the secret prison of self-contempt.

I wish we could all be so. If we could learn to like ourselves even a little, maybe our cruelties and angers might melt away. Maybe we would not have to hurt one another just to keep our ego chins above water.

On Love

BY

ERICH FROMM

AUTHOR OF "THE ART OF LOVING"

"There is only one kind of love,
but there are a thousand imitations."
—DUC DE LA ROCHEFOUCAULD

The deepest need of man is the need to overcome his separateness, to leave the prison of his aloneness. The full answer to the problem of existence lies in true and mature love.

What is mature love? It is union under the condition of preserving one's integrity, one's individuality. Love is an active power in man, a power which breaks through the walls which separate man from his fellow men, which unites him with others. Love makes him overcome the sense of isolation and separateness, yet it permits him to be himself. In love the paradox occurs that two beings become one and yet remain two.

A World to Love

BY

ETHEL BARRYMORE

BELOVED ACTRESS OF STAGE AND SCREEN

"Oh, earth, you're too wonderful for anybody to realize you.
Do any human beings ever realize life while they live it—
every, every minute?"
—THORNTON WILDER, EMILY IN "OUR TOWN"

You must learn day by day, year by year, to broaden your horizon. The more things you love, the more you are interested in, the more you enjoy, the more you are indignant about—the more you have left when anything happens.

I suppose the greatest thing in the world is loving people and wanting to destroy the sin but not the sinner. And not to forget that when life knocks you to your knees—well, that's the best position in which to pray, isn't it? On your knees. That's where I learned.

EDITOR'S NOTE: *Ethel Barrymore, who died in 1959 at the age of 79, brought more than a commanding presence and faultless technique to her long, distinguished theatrical career. She was a woman of rare insight and understanding, as this expression of her personal philosophy so eloquently reveals.*

Blessed Boomerang

BY

MAURICE CHEVALIER

COMEDIAN

"The days that make us happy make us wise."
—JOHN MASEFIELD

People are all the time asking me one question: "How do you always manage to be so cheerful?"

Of course I do not always feel gay. If I did I would be what you call "slap-happy." But immediately when I sense an audience responding to the gaiety I am trying to give out, I feel gaiety coming back to me. It is like a boomerang—a blessed boomerang.

This works not only for the performer. It is a good game anybody can play.

A man goes to his office. He is grumpy, growls a greeting to his secretary. She may have awakened spirited and jaunty, but right away the ugliness is contagious. Or, in reverse, he comes in whistling. Maybe he has picked a flower from his garden for his buttonhole as he hurried to catch his train. He extends a merry greeting, it boomerangs. The office brightens.

There are targets everywhere. Just take aim and let go with good cheer.

I like to try it out on bus drivers in big cities. They are a worried lot. People ask them long and involved questions, usually about how to get some place in the opposite direction. So board a bus, give a greeting. One time it did not work. I was not in a good mood. My approach, or rather my aim, was poor. The driver snarled, whether in pain or indifference I do not know. Then I transferred to another bus. This time I threw out the greeting with urgency and determination. My greeting was returned, wrapped in a pleasant smile. I got off that bus revived.

The business of getting back something for what you give appeals to my practical French nature, especially when the "something" benefits you so much. It is what they call in business a high rate of return.

So, Happy Hunting—or perhaps I should say Happy Boomeranging!

"But I Like You"

BY

MYLES CONNOLLY

AUTHOR OF
"THE BUMP ON BRANNIGAN'S HEAD"

---

*"Lord, make me an Instrument of Thy Peace. Where there
is hatred, let me sow love. Where there is injury, pardon . . ."*
—ST. FRANCIS OF ASSISI

The game of Cowboys and Indians had been going on vigorously
and, to stretch the meaning of the word a little, peacefully, out on the
beach for some time. Then, suddenly, there was trouble.

One of the youngsters, a brown-haired Cowboy, about seven and the
youngest of the lot, had been captured by the Indians and was to be tied
to a stake—the stake being a huge, ugly hunk of driftwood that looked
very much like the gnarled roots of an ancient tree. The brown-haired
Cowboy objected to being tied to the driftwood. Whether, in his con-
cept of the game, the driftwood was not legitimately a stake or whether
he, out of some special sensitivity, found the ugly driftwood objection-
able, I could not make out. But he was very definite about it. He would
not be tied to it.

The boss of the game, the oldest of the boys, about ten or eleven and
something of a bully, grew angry.

"Go on home, Yellow!" he shouted at the little fellow, "Go on
home. We don't like you!"

The other boys, in the natural spirit of the gang, took up the words
in a sort of singsong. "Go on home, Yellow! We don't like you!"

The boy, hurt and bewildered by this sudden show of cruelty, looked
from one face to another. Then, after a long moment, in a voice
quavering but deeply earnest, he said, "But I like you."

The singsong stopped before his earnestness. For a brief moment,
it seemed as if his simple but gravely moving words would have some
effect. Three of the boys looked at one another in uncertainty. They
had been somehow touched.

But the bully had not been touched. "Go on home, Yellow!" he cried out again. And then to the gang, "Come on, fellers! Let's go!"

The game was begun again without the brown-haired Cowboy.

He looked desolately on for a minute or two, then turned and moved slowly away, following the frothing white line of the sea's edge, sadness in his drooping figure, bewilderment still on his sensitive face.

I watched him go. I felt profoundly sorry for him. It was as if I had just watched the stoning of a prophet.

He grew smaller in the distance. Still his words stayed with me.

"But I like you."

It is a long way from a mountain in Galilee to the beach at Malibu and today's world, yet that brown-haired boy, standing there on the sand, answering his young tormentors with an earnest declaration of his affection for them, vividly brought back to me those dramatic, revolutionary words, "But I say unto you, love your enemies . . . ."

He disappeared from my view around a wide sweep of the shore.

What would the years do to the little Cowboy? Could he go on saying to his enemies, "But I like you?" Could it ever be he would remain unspoiled in the world and one day be a saint?

⚜

On Staying Young

B Y

DOUGLAS MacARTHUR

GENERAL OF THE UNITED STATES ARMY

EDITOR'S NOTE: *General MacArthur chose the following quotation as his Words to Live By, early in the Pacific War. Wherever his headquarters, he placed over his desk three frames—one a portrait of Washington; one a portrait of Lincoln; and between them, the message printed below. It is based on a passage which appeared originally in the book "From the Summit of Years Four Score," by Samuel Ullman of Birmingham, Alabama:*

"Youth is not a time of life; it is a state of mind; it is not a matter of rosy cheeks, red lips and supple knees; it is a matter of the will, a quality of the imagination, a vigor of the emotions; it is the freshness of the deep springs of life.

"Youth means the predominance of courage over timidity, of adventure over the love of ease. This often exists in a man of sixty more than in a boy of twenty. Nobody grows old merely by a number of years. We grow old by deserting our ideals.

"Years may wrinkle the skin, but to give up enthusiasm wrinkles the soul. Worry, doubt, self-distrust, fear and despair—these bow the heart and turn the spirit back to dust.

"Whether sixty or sixteen, there is in every human being's heart the love of wonder, the sweet amazement at the stars and the starlike things, the undaunted challenge of events, the unfailing child-like appetite for what-next, and the joy of the game of living.

"You are as young as your faith, as old as your doubt; as young as your self-confidence, as old as your fear; as young as your hope, as old as your despair."

Enthusiasm

BY

SAMUEL GOLDWYN

FAMOUS HOLLYWOOD PRODUCER

"Nothing great was ever achieved without enthusiasm."
—RALPH WALDO EMERSON

Emerson was certainly right—but not right enough. For enthusiasm is the key not only to the achievement of great things but to the accomplishment of anything that is worth while.

Enthusiasm is a wonderful word. But more, it is a wonderful feeling. It is a way of life. It is a magic spark that transforms "being" into "living." It makes hard work easy—and enjoyable. There is no better tonic for depression, no greater elixir for whatever happens to be wrong at the moment, than enthusiasm.

No person who is enthusiastic about his work has anything to fear from life. All the opportunities in the world—and they are as plentiful today as ever despite what some people say—are waiting to be grasped by the people who are in love with what they are doing.

For as long as I can remember, whatever I was doing at the time was the most important thing in the world to me. Today I look forward to my next picture with the same degree of excitement and anticipation and enthusiasm with which I went into my very first production.

I have found enthusiasm for work and life to be the most precious ingredient in any recipe for successful living. And the greatest feature of this ingredient is that it is available to everyone—within himself.

"Oh, Those Days of Childhood!"

BY

GRANDMA MOSES

ARTIST AND CENTENARIAN

"Happiness follows simplicity."
—IRISH PROVERB

In the springtime of life there is aplenty to do. Oh, those damp snowy days, early in spring, when we loved to go to the woods, and look for the first bloom of the trailing arbutus, which sometimes blooms beneath the snow, or gather the pussy willows. Feeling nearer to God's intentions, nearer to nature. Where in some respects, we are free, where there is beauty and tranquility, where we sometimes long to be, quiet and undisturbed, free from the hubbub of life.

Haying time on the farm, when they gather the grain, fruit and berries of all description, and the little folks gather the eggs. When the church picnic comes, and the children can have all the cake and lemonade they want, water melon and peanuts, what a wonderful treat!

And the fall of the year, and there are many odd jobs to attend to, food to be stored away for the coming cold weather, the ground to be plowed for rye and other crops before it is frozen hard. Ditches to dig. Poultry to cull and house.

Thanksgiven, in some homes there will be rejoicing, in others there will be sorrow. But we that can give thanks, should, there is so much to be thankful for, and praise God for all blessings, and the abundance of all things.

And then wintertime! When zero stands at 25 or 30, when we cannot deny the pleasure of skating till we have bumped heads, and bleedy noses, and the ice is like glass. Oh what joy and pleasure as we get together, to go for the Christmas tree, what aircastles we build as we slide down the hill, who can rebuild what we see on that Christmas tree?

Oh, those days of childhood!

Imagination

BY

MARY MARTIN

"Every wish is like a prayer to God."
—ELIZABETH BARRETT BROWNING

If I had the magic gift of Tinker Bell, I'd flit into the minds of my friends and leave this prescription for happiness: Stop the habit of wishful thinking and start the habit of thoughtful wishes. I would sweep away all those dreary office desk signs that say "Think" for another batch that shout "Wish!" Wishes are thoughts vibrant with life and eager for action. They have the power to produce light and beauty.

Personally I am almost afraid of the power in a wish, so many of mine have come true. As a little girl in Weatherford, Texas, I had five giant wishes. First, I wanted to fly—not aviator style, but like an angel. Second, as I emerged from pigtails, I wanted to marry a "wonderful guy" and have two children. I also wanted to sing to the world. I hankered to live in a house on a tree-covered hill in some faraway land. And, above all, I yearned to perform on a London stage with my idol, Noel Coward, whom I had seen at the local movie house in *The Scoundrel.*

My wish to fly stuck hauntingly with me into adulthood. At least once a week I'd dream I was airborne under my own power. One night I had a vivid dream of flying into New York through the Holland Tunnel. How I managed to sail over the long stream of trucks and cars, without hitting the ceiling, only Freud knows.

Soon after that I received a telegram offering me the role of Peter Pan on Broadway. During its long run I did a heap of "flying" angel style. And the funny thing is that never have I dreamed of flying again.

One night after my premiere in *One Touch of Venus,* several years ago, I was dining late at an intimate, dimly lit restaurant near

13

the theater. A man I had never met emerged from the shadows, passed my table, bent down and kissed my forehead.

"You were wonderful," he said.

It was Noel Coward. Four years later I went to London to star in *Pacific 1860,* a musical he wrote especially for his worshiper from Weatherford.

The blessing of the "wonderful guy" and the two children has also come my way. And we've bought a house on a hillside in Brazil where we can all be together. Nowadays, I watch my wishes like a hawk.

What is true of me applies to everyone. It's a wonderful custom to extend best wishes to our friends at New Year's. But, more important, let's be sure to extend best wishes to ourselves—wish them to ourselves with all our heart and strive toward them with all our might.

If you're willing to do that, select your wishes with care. For they have an uncanny way of coming true!

Something More

BY

ALBERT SCHWEITZER

DOCTOR, CLERGYMAN,
AND MEDICAL MISSIONARY

---

*"Thou shalt love the Lord thy God with all thy heart, and
with all thy soul, and with all thy mind. This is the first
and great commandment. And the second is like unto it,
Thou shalt love thy neighbor as thyself."*
—MATTHEW 22:37-39

It is not enough merely to exist. It's not enough to say, "I'm earning
enough to live and to support my family. I do my work well. I'm a
good father. I'm a good husband. I'm a good churchgoer."

That's all very well. *But you must do something more.*
Seek always to do some good, somewhere. Every man has to seek in his
own way to make his own self more noble and to realize his own true
worth.

You must give some time to your fellow man. Even if it's a little
thing, do something for those who have need of a man's help, something for which you get no pay but the privilege of doing it. For remember, you don't live in a world all your own. *Your brothers are
here, too.*

ON
BEING
AND
DOING

On Courage

B Y

J. EDGAR HOOVER

DIRECTOR OF THE F.B.I.

"He that loses wealth loses much:
But he that loses courage loses all."
—CERVANTES

Cervantes' words affirm that courage is a priceless ingredient of character. The will to do, the tenacity to overcome all obstacles and finish the course, the strength to cling to inexorable ideals are rooted in courage. It is the outward manifestation of our spiritual development.

I have never seen a courageous criminal. True, some exhibit bravado behind a gun or in the protection of overwhelming numbers, but that is not real courage. I am speaking of the kind which is vital to the preservation and perpetuation of a free nation: the mental and moral courage which drives us to seek truth. It is the kind which enables us to stand by our convictions, to uphold right for the sake of right. It was this courage which built America. This is the high courage we must develop as pioneers of the Atomic Age. In Cervantes' words lie both a challenge and a warning.

On Courtesy

BY

FRANK S. HOGAN

DISTRICT ATTORNEY OF NEW YORK COUNTY

"Hail the small sweet courtesies of life,
for smooth do they make the road of it."
—LAURENCE STERNE

Courteous treatment is a recognition by one person that another person has the same dignity as a human being. The practice of courtesy develops the habit of treating others as equals. It is, therefore, more than a lubricant which prevents irritation between individuals of different backgrounds. It becomes a solvent of the causes of friction and, when constantly applied, produces a positive force in the creation of good will.

Is that a little thing? If so, life is full of little things—full of small pains and petty grievances which little remedies can cure.

It was a little thing which caused the first brothers to quarrel. Abel, you remember, had killed a lamb and brought it as a sacrifice to Jehovah. Cain, in turn, placed some grain on his own altar. The lamb was the more acceptable offering. Cain thought Abel was laughing at him. Abel denied it. Then Cain asked his brother to go away. Abel refused. Whereupon Cain hit Abel. But he hit him too hard, and Abel fell dead.

Fully half of the cases in our criminal courts, where the offense is against the person, originate in little things. Barroom bravado, domestic wrangling, an insulting remark, a disparaging word, a rude action—those are the little things that lead to assault and murder.

Very few of us are cruelly and greatly wronged. It is the small blows to our self-esteem, the indignities, the little jolts to our vanity which cause half the heartaches in the world.

If ordinary civility, the courtesy we expect to be shown, were extended to every person with whom we come in contact in our daily lives, would it not be a real contribution to human brotherhood?

On Pride

BY

INGRID BERGMAN

STAGE AND SCREEN STAR

"Look out how you use proud words.
When you let proud words go, it is not easy to call them
  back.
They wear long boots, hard boots . . .
Look out how you use proud words."
—CARL SANDBURG

There is in these words a primary lesson for individuals and classes and nations alike. All too often, we say the cruel and destructive things— because it is so much easier to be clever than to be kind. But in the long run, proud and angry words are the ones which cause trouble in our homes, our communities, and among nations.

Proud words are arrogant, intolerant, and savagely ignorant of the great fundamental truths—simplicity, humility, and ordinary human decency. They are indeed roughshod, and it is not easy to call them back.

Bravery

BY

GENERAL MAXWELL D. TAYLOR

CHIEF OF STAFF, U. S. ARMY

"He either fears his fate too much,
Or his deserts are small,
That dares not put it to the touch,
To gain or lose it all."

—MARQUIS OF MONTROSE

These lines from the seventeenth-century Marquis of Montrose have special meaning for me because of the way in which I first heard them.

The greatest military operation of history was the Allied invasion of Normandy in June 1944. Probably no other operation ever received such careful planning and meticulous attention to its smallest requirements. For months the training areas, airfields and ports of Great Britain hummed with the activity of soldiers, sailors and airmen. Important phases of the invasion plan were rehearsed in great maneuvers which reproduced with all possible realism the conditions anticipated in combat.

As D Day approached, the senior commanders assembled their principal subordinates for a final review of the plans. The largest conference of this kind was held in St. Paul's School in London under the monitorship of Field Marshal Montgomery. Here the Allied commanders of all the services consulted together and verified the readiness of their preparations.

After a long day of earnest discussions, as the meeting was about to adjourn, Marshal Montgomery arose and gave a final address in which he expressed his confidence in the success of this great enterprise. In closing, he commended to us the words of Montrose I have quoted. They were with me on D Day in Normandy and have been with me ever since as a spur to decisive action when the cards are down.

I stress the importance of the context, because in themselves these words might be taken simply as poetic counsel to a rash willingness to "shoot the works." But with the background of our careful preparations for Normandy, they become a rejection of fear of failure after every preparation has been made and every contingency anticipated.

Assuming such preparations, these words say that there are times in the lives of both men and nations when we must be willing to risk much in order to win much. They are a counsel against timidity and for the bold recognition of those great moments when we must be prepared to "let the chips fall where they may." In these troubled times we can exert effective leadership only if it is apparent to the whole world that there are certain things so important that, regardless of hazard, we dare to put all to the test, as becomes a people whose deserts are large.

Boldness

BY

JAMES A. MICHENER

AUTHOR OF

"TALES OF THE SOUTH PACIFIC"

---

*"Behold the turtle: He makes progress
only when he sticks his neck out."*
—JAMES BRYANT CONANT

These lively words of a famous scientist and educator have special meaning for me.

In 1944 I was stuck on a remote island in the South Pacific. To kill time I decided to write a book. Then I remembered the cold facts: The chances against anyone's publishing a first book are ninety-five to one; for each book that is finally published, ninety-five unsuccessful ones are written. But I decided to stick my neck out and go ahead.

Then I learned two more facts. If a man hasn't written a book by the time he's thirty-five years old, chances are he never will. And I was nearing forty. Even worse, I was not writing a novel but a book of short stories. A friend warned me, "Nobody publishes books of short stories any more." Even so, I still decided to stick my neck out. And it was then I found I was in good company.

When the book appeared, it seemed as if the prophecies of doom had been correct. My work caused little comment and would have died unknown except that Orville Prescott, a newspaper book reviewer, took a chance on a beginning writer and reported that he had liked the stories.

Later, a group of literary critics studied the book and pointed out, "It's not a novel, it's not about America, and common sense says it's not eligible for the Pulitzer Prize." Nevertheless they awarded it the prize and so brought the book to the world's attention.

In Hollywood, Kenneth MacKenna, who reads books for the movies, tried to persuade his company to make a movie out of *Tales of the South Pacific,* but the experts replied, "No dramatic possibilities."

So MacKenna stuck his neck out and brought the book to the attention of Richard Rodgers and Oscar Hammerstein II, who did likewise.

When Broadway heard that R & H planned a musical called *South Pacific*, wiseacres cried, "Have you heard their screwy idea? The romantic lead is gonna be a man past fifty. An opera singer named Ezio Pinza!" You know what happened next!

You can understand why I like people who stick their necks out.

Confidence

B Y

KONRAD ADENAUER

FEDERAL GERMAN CHANCELLOR

"Lift where you stand."
—EDWARD EVERETT

Most of us, in moments of fatigue or discouragement, have taken a look at our daily task and wondered, "What does it really matter?" Precisely at those moments we should tell ourselves what my lifetime has taught me is the one true answer: "I shall keep doing the job, for I matter a great deal."

Let me counsel young people who are ambitious that they can best get ahead by making themselves important in the job at hand. Then they will not have to look for the next higher job—it will be offered to them. In all humility, I was much too busy being mayor of my well-loved city of Cologne to waste time dreaming that some day my countrymen might ask me to be their Chancellor. Yet that day came.

When the world seems large and complex, we need to remember that great world ideals all begin in some home neighborhood. I doubt, for example, that the men of the Middle Ages who built Germany's famed free cities guessed how high they were building. They simply did the job at hand. Yet now we have their traditions of liberal self-government as a model for our free republic; those city planners set an example that has outlasted kaisers and dictators.

So history shows us that our moments of discouragement can become the moments for our new starts. When we put inspiration into raising our family, or do the shop work better than required, or make our town a model for others, then our influence spreads in widening circles. We are each more important than we think.

On Self-Respect

BY

PHYLLIS McGINLEY

PULITZER PRIZE POET,
AUTHOR OF ''TIMES THREE''

"Don't let your sins turn into bad habits."
—ST. TERESA OF AVILA

The woman I quote was one of the wittiest, holiest, most delightful creatures who ever lived. She was speaking to a nun of her order, an overscrupulous girl who came to her in tears, berating her own evil nature. "Ah, my dear," Teresa consoled her, "all of us are human and prone to sin. Just see to it that you don't let your sins turn into bad habits."

The paradox is as full of common sense as it is of the saint's famous salty humor. Certainly to err is human, and Teresa knew it as well as the poet Alexander Pope. It is not the occasional lapse but the repeated fault which turns us into the sort of persons we do not wish to be. We can all mourn a trouble. It's the habit of self-pity which corrodes character. To fly into a rage now and then is excusable. But to let a habit of anger master us is to court destruction. We all like gossip, it's the amusing small change of conversation. But a habit of malice can turn us into bores, troublemakers, monsters of mischief.

Few of us are murderers or traitors or thieves. Yet unkindness is a sin, too, and so is selfishness or intemperance or spite or hate or sloth or detraction. And how many of us are altogether free of those flaws? Wisdom lies in the ability to forgive ourselves such human failings— to tumble, pick ourselves up, shake the dust off our spirits, and try to avoid the next mistake.

No matter what degree of religious faith we profess, all of us yearn to be decent people and we believe in free will. Teresa has given us the best possible advice to follow on the thorny, difficult road to self-respect.

On Laughter

BY

GELETT BURGESS

HUMORIST AND AUTHOR OF "THE PURPLE COW"

---

*"Laffing iz the sensation ov pheeling good all over, and
showing it principally in one spot."*
—JOSH BILLINGS

The old professor I went to hear, that night in Paris, began his talk by commanding: "Laugh! Everybody in the audience laugh! Laugh out loud. That's it. Now louder! Louder!" One after another began to laugh, and soon the whole place was convulsed with uproarious laughter.

I hadn't felt much like laughing when I went in. Some people can laugh at their own troubles, but when one you love is suffering and you can do nothing to help, it's hard to show mirth. I had almost forgotten how to smile. But I laughed with the rest—I couldn't help it —and I went away feeling definitely happier.

Next day I saw, in a magazine, the picture of a sweepstakes winner. She was laughing all over. I pinned her to my wall and every time I looked at her I smiled. Every time, I felt better.

Then I began to cut out every laughing picture I could find in newspapers, magazines, advertisements. I finally filled a book with them. Not mere photographic smiles or smirks, though. You need genuine, ha-ha-ha laughter to stimulate merriment.

I showed my scrapbook to a nurse. She roared. In the hospital she gave it to a patient, and at sight of those laughing faces, he smiled for the first time in months. From bed to bed the book was passed, and in one ward after another the doctors testified that this laugh cure almost always produced a marked improvement. I made other scrapbooks; I sent them to discouraged or ailing friends, always with the same happy result.

Laughter is a real medicine. It has optimistic vitamins in it. It revives like oxygen. It restores failing morale. I have proved for myself the "cleansing power of laughter."

Don't Sneer at Nonsense

BY

JIMMY DURANTE

COMEDIAN

"A little nonsense now and then
Is relished by the wisest men."
—ANONYMOUS

The other night, after a very tough day at the studio, I try to get out of a dinner date. I say I'm too tired and grumpy to be good company. But the people insist I've got to show up anyway, since the lamb chops are already in the skillet. So I finally give in.

No sooner do I get in the door when my host says, "Jimmy, dinner's not quite ready and little Clara has been waiting for you to read to her before she goes to sleep." That's just what I need! In the mood I'm in, I'm supposed to go through a bedtime-story session with a four-year-old. But I am trapped, so I go upstairs and take the book the kid gives me and I start to read to her.

I soon get quite a surprise. It's been a long time since I read the wonderful nonsense about the Walrus that cries as he carves the oysters, the Elephant that plays the fife, the Pobble who has no toes, the Owl and the Pussycat which went to sea in a beautiful pea-green boat. I am soon getting as big a kick out of it as the little girl!

When I come downstairs I am all covered with smiles and ready to leap into those lamb chops. And it gets me to thinking, too—which is a feat in itself, folks. I think, Jimmy, nonsense is your stock in trade, but maybe you don't realize how healthy it is off the job.

Maybe there's nobody who is smart and wise enough to do without a little nonsense. Maybe it's even more important than ever these days, when the headlines are not the happiest which I ever read, to have a sort of safety valve.

When we were all kids, we grew up with nonsense as a sort of a friend. And I figure the guy who says to himself, "I've out-grown that sort of stuff," must be a pretty lonely guy.

29

Take a Chance

BY

WALT DISNEY

MOTION PICTURE PRODUCER

"In the lexicon of youth . . . there is no such word as fail!"
—EDWARD BULWER-LYTTON

I wonder how many times these sturdy old words have been used in graduation speeches each year. They take me back to my own high school days, when I had my first pair of white flannel trousers and the world ahead held no heartbreak or fear.

Certainly we have all had this confidence at one time in our lives, though most of us lose it as we grow older. Perhaps, because of my work, I've been lucky enough to retain a shred of this youthful quality. But sometimes, as I look back on how tough things were, I wonder if I'd go through it again. I hope I would.

When I was about twenty-one, I went broke for the first time. I slept on chair cushions in my "studio" in Kansas City and ate cold beans out of a can. But I took another look at my dream and set out for Hollywood.

Foolish? Not to a youngster. An older person might have had too much "common sense" to do it. Sometimes I wonder if "common sense" isn't another way of saying "fear." And "fear" too often spells failure.

In the lexicon of youth there is no such word as "fail." Remember the story about the boy who wanted to march in the circus parade? When the show came to town, the bandmaster needed a trombonist, so the boy signed up. He hadn't marched a block before the fearful noises from his horn caused two old ladies to faint and a horse to run away. The bandmaster demanded, "Why didn't you tell me you couldn't play the trombone?" And the boy said, "How did I know? I never tried before!"

Many years ago, I might have done just what that boy did. Now I'm a grandfather and have a good many gray hairs and what a lot of people would call common sense. But if I'm no longer young in age, I hope I stay young enough in spirit never to fear failure—young enough still to take a chance and march in the parade.

On Chills and Thrills

B Y

ALFRED HITCHCOCK

HOLLYWOOD AND TV MASTER OF SUSPENSE

"A tale which holdeth children from play and old men from the chimney-corner." —SIR PHILIP SIDNEY

The other day a fascinating statistic was brought to my notice. I was asked to believe that in a single year some 40,000,000 prescriptions will have been written for tranquilizers to relieve the tensions of the world Americans live in. Now, I have no quarrel with any sort of medication. But I believe I have a more pleasing prescription:

Take a suspense story . . . quake well . . . and keep quaking!

From the days when legends of bold deeds and sudden death were sung by minstrels, the suspense story has enraptured audiences and made them forget for a little while the problems of their own lives. To hold a man spellbound for an hour is to return him refreshed to face to-morrow.

Of course the world of the suspense story is a world of make believe. Of course it is what the critics call "escape." But is that bad? These are entertainments, designed to take you out of yourself, to make you believe while you read, or look at a screen, in the reality of what is there. When it is over, when the criminal is properly trapped and you are returned to your private worries, you find that your little excursion has made your mind clearer, your nerves calmer, your problems somehow easier to attack.

For some troubled persons I have no doubt that the siesta on the psychiatrist's couch is a necessity. But for a good many others who are disturbed by tension, my magic potion can have healing effect.

This little homily is designed to free you of any guilty conscience from indulging in the pure entertainment of a suspense story. You may relax and enjoy the chills and thrills. As a tension reliever, they are just what the doctor ordered. And if they help you to be a calmer, better, happier person, then I shall feel that my labors in the field of crime have not altogether been in vain.

ON
SEEING
THINGS
CLEARLY

On Having Fun

BY

DONALD CULROSS PEATTIE

AUTHOR AND NATURALIST

"If your morals make you dreary,
depend upon it they are wrong."
—ROBERT LOUIS STEVENSON

I have long been delighted by this warning from the gallant prophet of the lively creed which declares that to be happy, if you possibly can, is a first duty to others. How the world has suffered from the dreary moralists, those gloomy souls who want to make other people good, rather than happy! They have darkened the lives of children with threats of hell-fire, hanged the witches at Salem, and persecuted thousands. Today, they counsel paralyzing doubt in a world that desperately needs strength of heart.

Stevenson's words do not mean that if your life is dull you must abandon moral standards and seek happiness in self-indulgence. But they do remind us that true goodness is a joyful thing. Men of true morality proclaim courage and gladness, and rouse in us the rapture of living. St. Francis of Assisi, Mozart, Audubon, Don Marquis—there springs to mind a motley company of fellows who knew how to minister to the world, and yet call up from it a laugh and a light heart.

The wind running through the grass, the thrush in the treetops, and children tumbling in senseless mirth stir in us a bright faith in life. It is heresy to turn from them with a frown. Dreary moralizing is poison in a cup of holy water. To live that way is to live by fear, not love. It is to think less of heaven than of hell. Indeed, I believe it is the cardinal irreverence.

On Thinking

BY

HELEN KELLER

DEAF AND BLIND
AUTHOR AND LECTURER

"I think, therefore I am."
—DESCARTES

Mine has been the limited experience of one who lives in a world without color and without sound. But ever since my student days I have had a joyous certainty that my physical handicaps were not an essential part of my being, since they were not in any way a part of my mind. This faith was confirmed when I came to Descartes' maxim, "I think, therefore I am."

Those five emphatic words waked something in me that has never slept since. I knew then that my mind could be a positive instrument of happiness, bridging over the dark, silent void with concepts of a vibrant, light-flooded happiness. I learned that it is possible for us to create light and sound and order within us, no matter what calamity may befall us in the outer world.

Starting Out

BY

WILLIAM SAROYAN

AUTHOR AND PLAYWRIGHT

"It is not impossible to walk on water."
—GARABED SAROYAN

These words were said to me about twenty-five years ago by my great-uncle Garabed Saroyan when he came into my bed-living-and-work room in a house in Fresno, California, where I had recently installed a typewriter.

I was almost thirteen at the time and he was an old man. I thought he was as old as any man could be, although he was probably well under sixty.

He said, "My boy, what is that contraption?"

I said, "It is a typewriter, sir."

"What is it for?" he said.

"It is for clear writing," I said, and handed him an example of typewriter-print on paper.

"What is this writing on the paper?"

"Philosophical sayings."

"By which philosopher?" my great-uncle Garabed said.

"By myself," I said.

He sat on the bed, lighted a cigarette, then studied the sheet of paper and his great-nephew.

When he got up to go he said, "Proceed, for it is not impossible to walk on water."

Even though he had said very little, there was no mistaking what he meant. Coming from him, a man famous for his fierce wit, this was approval, recognition, and encouragement to keep on trying, and I felt much obliged to him.

Keeping Going

B Y

CORNELIA OTIS SKINNER

ACTRESS-MONOLOGIST AND CO-AUTHOR OF
"OUR HEARTS WERE YOUNG AND GAY"

"This day we sailed on. Course WSW."
—CHRISTOPHER COLUMBUS

This was the entry which, day after day, Columbus put down in the private log of his first voyage across the uncharted North Atlantic. He must have written it in a spirit alternating between blind hope and quiet despair.

Conditions were about as adverse as possible. Storms had damaged the little caravel; the *Pinta* had lost her rudder; the crews of all three vessels were threatening mutiny; and probably Columbus' own confidence in what seemed an insane enterprise was wavering. But he had intelligence led him to believe was the right one, and with dogged set his course in the direction which his own intuition and logical courage he kept on going.

The words are not especially comforting ones, but these are days when the world is less in need of supine comfort than of high gallantry and faith in an inner integrity. During times of distress, doubt and weariness, people may well be inspirited by the words of the great navigator, "This day we sailed on."

Face and Fortune

BY

FRANCES PARKINSON KEYES

AUTHOR OF ''CAME A CAVALIER''
AND ''DINNER AT ANTOINE'S''

"To thine own self be true."
—SHAKESPEARE

There is a story about a proposed appointment in Lincoln's cabinet that I have always liked very much. One of his advisers urgently recommended a candidate and Lincoln declined to follow the suggestion. So he was asked to give his reasons.

"I don't like the man's face," Lincoln explained briefly.

"But the poor man is not responsible for his face," his advocate insisted.

"Every man over forty is responsible for his face," Lincoln replied, and turned to the discussion of other matters.

Recently, at the instigation of my publisher, I had some photographs taken. It was a long time, he reminded me, since I had supplied him with a new one; I could not go on using the same pose indefinitely. I do not enjoy the process of being photographed, and when I saw the results of this latest ordeal, I enjoyed these still less. I compared the new photograph with one that had been taken twenty-five years ago, and my feminine vanity suffered an acute pang at the thought of being presented to the public as I am today. My first instinct was to have the prints "touched up," though I have never "touched up" my own face or my own hair because I have always maintained that women who did this deceived no one except themselves. As I thoughtfully considered the photographs, I knew that a still more important principle was involved.

A quarter century of living should put a great deal into a woman's face besides a few wrinkles and some unwelcome folds around the chin. In that length of time she has become intimately acquainted with pain and pleasure, joy and sorrow, life and death. She has struggled and survived, failed and succeeded. She has lost and regained faith. And, as a result, she should be wiser, gentler, more patient and more tolerant than she was when she was young. Her sense of humor should have mellowed, her outlook should have widened, her sympathies should have deepened. And all this should show. If she tries to erase the imprint of age, she runs the risk of destroying, at the same time, the imprint of experience and character.

I know I am more experienced than I was a quarter century ago and I hope I have more character. I released the pictures as they were.

On Motes and Beams

BY

W. SOMERSET MAUGHAM

AUTHOR OF "OF HUMAN BONDAGE"

"How seldom we weigh our neighbor
in the same balance with ourselves."
—THOMAS À KEMPIS

It is curious that our own offenses should seem so much less heinous than the offenses of others. I suppose the reason is that we know all the circumstances that have occasioned them and so manage to excuse in ourselves what we cannot excuse in others. We turn our attention away from our own defects, and when we are forced by untoward events to consider them, find it easy to condone them. For all I know we are right to do this; they are part of us and we must accept the good and bad in ourselves together.

But when we come to judge others, it is not by ourselves as we really are that we judge them, but by an image that we have formed of ourselves from which we have left out everything that offends our vanity or would discredit us in the eyes of the world. To take a trivial instance: how scornful we are when we catch someone out telling a lie; but who can say that he has never told not one, but a hundred?

There is not much to choose between men. They are all a hotchpotch of greatness and littleness, of virtue and vice, of nobility and baseness. Some have more strength of character, or more opportunity, and so in one direction or another give their instincts freer play, but potentially they are the same. For my part, I do not think I am any better or any worse than most people, but I know that if I set down every action in my life and every thought that has crossed my mind, the world would consider me a monster of depravity. The knowledge that these reveries are common to all men should inspire one with tolerance to oneself as well as to others. It is well also if they enable us to look upon our fellows, even the most eminent and respectable, with humor, and if they lead us to take ourselves not too seriously.

On Being Right

BY

WILLIAM NICHOLS

EDITOR OF "THIS WEEK" MAGAZINE

---

*"There's a Harvard man on the wrong side
of every question."*
—A. LAWRENCE LOWELL

When I was a boy I used to think that somewhere out ahead lay a magic moment when one would be grown up, and know all the answers. At that point life would be easy: no more doubts, no more uncertainties. In any given situation, one would always know exactly what to do.

Since then, many years have gone by, and the only thing I have really learned is that the moment of absolute certainty never comes. Along the way, while looking for the answers, I had the treat of knowing the late president of Harvard, A. Lawrence Lowell. Some of his salty sayings were better than a college degree.

Once, for example, he said: "There's a Harvard man on the wrong side of every question." It was his way of making the point that each of us is different and that no one can ever know all the answers all the time.

Another of his favorite sayings went this way: "The mark of an educated man is the ability to make a reasoned guess on the basis of insufficient information."

What can we infer from Lowell's observations? Simply this: that often, when a man is faced with a decision, it is impossible for him to fill in all the uncertainties. He cannot be *sure* he has every fact. And so, in deciding, he must guess. But this is precisely the point at which "education" comes in. For true education goes far beyond facts. It means more than classrooms and lectures and examinations. Education also means *experience* and *faith, courage* and *understanding.* Most of all it means *the ability to think and act.* These are the qualities which translate dead knowledge into living wisdom. They are what make our "guesses" turn out right.

Two Kinds of People

B Y

ROGER HULL

BUSINESS EXECUTIVE

"If everyone swept his own doorstep,
then the whole wide world would be clean."
—PROVERB

Have you ever asked yourself this question: If every citizen performed just as you do, where would the country be? What if every fellow worked at his job the way you work, showed the same interest, the same diligence, the same faithfulness, the same skill and discipline? What would happen to our country?

Someone has aptly said that there are really only two kinds of people: those who are part of the problem and those who are part of the solution.

Well, what about you?

Do you think only in terms of yourself—how much you can make, what you can get out of life? Those who think that way are definitely part of the problem.

Or are you concerned with the contribution you can make—how much you can give, how much you can put in? People like that are part of the answer.

Some people treat life like a slot machine, trying to put in as little as possible, and always hoping to hit the jackpot. But I believe that people are wiser, happier, and have more inner peace when they think of life as a solid, intelligent investment from which they receive in terms of what they put in. And by so doing they help preserve our free society.

Ideas

BY

JOHN DEWEY

PHILOSOPHER AND TEACHER

"When men have realized that time has upset many fighting faiths, they may come to believe that the ultimate good is better reached by free trade in ideas."
—OLIVER WENDELL HOLMES

There never has been a time when it was as important as it is today to take into our heads the spirit that inspires these words. In a time of extreme distress and uncertainty, we reach out blindly for some final and finished truth. Justice Holmes reminds us that truth is a matter of never-ending search. In a time of longing for external authority, he reminds us that the open mind, manifested in free search and free discussion, is the sole method of conducting the search with safety and assurance. In a time when reasonableness and intelligence are undergoing eclipse, he reminds us that fact, discovered by continued inquiry, is in the long run the only ground upon which realization of human desires can be attained.

On Peace of Mind

BY

JOSHUA LOTH LIEBMAN

CLERGYMAN AND AUTHOR OF
''PEACE OF MIND''

---

*"On my head pour only the sweet waters of serenity.
Give me the gift of the Untroubled Mind."*

Once, as a young man full of exuberant fancy, I undertook to draw up
a catalogue of the acknowledged "goods" of life. As other men sometimes tabulate lists of properties they own or would like to own, I
set down my inventory of earthly desirables: health, love, beauty, talent,
power, riches, and fame.

When my inventory was completed I proudly showed it to a wise
elder who had been the mentor and spiritual model of my youth. Perhaps I was trying to impress him with my precocious wisdom. Anyway,
I handed him the list. "This," I told him confidently, "is the sum of
mortal goods. Could a man possess them all, he would be as a god."

At the corners of my friend's old eyes, I saw wrinkles of amusement
gathering in a patient net. "An excellent list," he said, pondering it
thoughtfully. "Well digested in content and set down in not-unrea-
sonable order. But it appears, my young friend, that you have omitted
the most important element of all. You have forgotten the one ingredient, lacking which, each possession becomes a hideous torment."

"And what," I asked, peppering my voice with truculence, "is that
missing ingredient?"

With a pencil stub he crossed out my entire schedule. Then, having
demolished my adolescent dream structure at a single stroke, he wrote
down three syllables: peace of mind. "This is the gift that God reserves
for His special proteges," he said.

"Talent and beauty He gives to many. Wealth is commonplace, fame
not rare. But peace of mind—that is His final guerdon of approval, the
fondest insignia of His love. He bestows it charily. Most men are never

45

blessed with it; others wait all their lives—yes, far into advanced age—for this gift to descend upon them."

He scanned the doubt on my young forehead. "This is no private opinion of mind," he explained. "I am merely paraphrasing from the Psalmists, Marcus Aurelius, and Lao-tse. 'God,' says each of these wise ones, 'heaps worldly gifts at the feet of foolish men. But on my head pour only the sweet waters of serenity. Give me the gift of the Untroubled Mind.'"

On Facing Life

BY

DOROTHY VAN DOREN

EDITOR AND AUTHOR

"I would finish hoeing my garden."
—ST. FRANCIS OF ASSISI

These words were St. Francis' answer when someone asked him, while working in his garden, what he would do if he were suddenly to learn that he would die at sunset that day.

They seem to me an answer to all the troubled young people these days who are beginning life in a world that appears to hold no security for them or for anyone, young or old.

Why should they bother to go to college when the atom war is just around the corner? Why should a young wife have a baby when the ceiling may collapse on its crib? Why should one paint a picture or write a song or begin a novel?

We can't be sure of anything, these young people say, not now, or next year, or the year after that. Why should we try to make a life for ourselves, they ask. Why should we go to classes or take examinations or get married or look for an apartment or try for a job? Next spring, or some spring too frighteningly near, it may all go, the life we have begun. Our world is in deadly peril, we have lost the promise of tomorrow.

St. Francis put the answer in a simple metaphor: go on hoeing your garden. The task is still here—the house to build, the book to write, the examination to prepare for. If the future looks dark, so did it on the morning before the first Christmas—and in the year 5,000 B.C. And however dark it seems today, however dark it is, we shall meet life better if we have fulfilled the present to the best of our ability. Today is still ours, along with the obligation to live it to the full. As St. Francis said, we must go on hoeing our garden.

The Mood

B Y

LILY PONS

OPERA STAR

"The ideal man is his own best friend
and takes delight in privacy."
—ARISTOTLE

American people are becoming more and more like the Red Queen in
Alice in Wonderland, who had to keep running in order to stay where
she was. The hectic tempo and mass activity of the business world have
spread into all phases of modern life. People have forgotten how to slow
down, how to be alone.

How often, during the furious activity of the week, we think of
all the things we will accomplish on the week end . . . reading a book
we have long heard about, taking care of unfinished correspondence,
putting our houses—literally and figuratively—in order. But when the
week end arrives, we find ourselves hurrying to parties to which we do
not really want to go, being swept up by a dozen social obligations.
Finally there is nothing left to the week end but the beginning of
another working week.

But the "ideal man" whom Aristotle described, indeed, the healthy
man in this or any other generation, allows himself some time for his
own thoughts. He is able to behave as a social being when he is in
society, but he is not afraid of his own company. He knows that each
day he must give some time to contemplation—that is, to looking
over his actions of the day and comparing them with his intentions,
making constructive plans for the future and simply being himself.

The problem, of course, is where to find the time or the place to be
alone. Singers and musicians are fortunate, for their work compels
them to take time to study and practice, and time to rest before per-
formances or concerts.

If musicians find such relaxation a help, then I think men and women
in the business world would too. Take a little time before that next

conference to let your mind run away from office cares. Break the boredom of a routine job, now and then, with a few minutes of "escape" thinking. If you have time left over after lunch, take a walk and let your mind be free—perhaps for a daydream, perhaps for a prayer.

Privacy of this sort can be found by any man. And each of us must find it if he is to remain a consistent and sane individual with a normal, happy inner life.

On Leadership

BY

DWIGHT D. EISENHOWER

FORMER CHIEF OF STAFF, U. S. A.

"The discipline which makes the soldiers of a free country reliable in battle is not to be gained by harsh or tyrannical treatment. On the contrary, such treatment is far more likely to destroy than to make an army. It is possible to give commands in such manner as to inspire an intense desire to obey; while the opposite manner cannot fail to excite strong resentment and a desire to disobey."
—MAJOR GENERAL JOHN M. SCHOFIELD

The words above have meaning to every man who has ever served in the armed forces of the United States. They express the spirit which should always guide the leaders in the armies of a free nation. They were first spoken in an address at West Point in August, 1887. By the time I was a cadet in 1911 they had been cast on a bronze tablet at an entrance to old South Barracks where they could be seen daily by passing cadets—and every plebe was required to memorize them. These are literally, the "Words to Live By" of the U.S. Army, and the great leaders are the ones who have lived up to them.

Magical Poetry

BY

SINCLAIR LEWIS

NOBEL PRIZE WINNER

It is healthy for one's sense of noble prose to quote the great words of a Thoreau, a Lincoln, a Plato—yet for guidance in living, those words frequently boil down to nothing more novel than "Be decent and generous, and the world and you will be happier." But you cannot be decent, you certainly cannot be generous to other people in their way, unless you have a mature imagination. And neither the sagest advice nor the whole cyclopedia of facts will cultivate that imagination as will these lines of poetry which are pure magic:

> *"A rose-red city, half as old as time."*
> —JOHN WILLIAM BURGON, "PETRA"

> *"... delight of battle with my peers*
> *Far on the ringing plains of windy Troy."*
> —TENNYSON, "ULYSSES"

> *"Charm'd magic casements, opening on the foam*
> *Of perilous seas, in faery lands forlorn."*
> —KEATS, "ODE TO A NIGHTINGALE"

> *"A savage place! as holy and enchanted*
> *As e'er beneath a waning moon was haunted*
> *By woman wailing for her demon lover!"*
> —COLERIDGE, "KUBLA KAHN"

Lines like these can never be too familiar! If you read them often enough to comprehend them, they are enchantments which lead on your imagination so that it perceives not only your own street, but all the streets and valleys and oceans in the world. They are keys that open the minds of all men—when you have learned how to turn them. It does not vastly matter whether you "know what they mean." Like music, they mean something beyond words and sense—something emotional and holy—and in the atomic age we need such holiness as well as the shrewdness of Franklin, the courage of Jefferson.

The Happiest Man

BY

DAVID NIVEN

MOTION PICTURE ACTOR

"It all balances."
—FRANK GOODALL

The happiest man I've ever known was a fisherman named Frank Goodall on the Isle of Wight, off the southern coast of England. He never set foot in our house there, but he had more to do with bringing me up than anyone—a sort of substitute father.

My father had been killed at the Dardanelles in 1915, and Mother was left with four of us. She was French, splendid, and very vague. Now suddenly we were augmented by a disastrous stepfather. He took a pretty dim view of all of us, but he detested me and I was packed off to boarding school at six.

Those were the days of the great bullies in English public schools, the days, too, of shell-shocked masters with a sad, sadistic streak. When at the age of seven, I couldn't master a Latin conjugation, I was stuck out of a fourth-floor classroom window and the window closed down on my back while I was soundly thrashed.

But summers and Easter vacation I went home to the Isle of Wight and told old Frank, the fisherman, all about it. Many as my problems were, with his help I managed to laugh them off. He taught me to fish, to catch lobster by hand, all the love of nature that has stood me in good stead ever since.

But above all, he gave me a piece of advice that has come to bear time and again on my adult life. He said, "I've been fishing for fifty years. You have a run of luck, then some days you'll have nothing, not even a nibble. It all balances." He couldn't have given me more needed wisdom.

I've remembered his words many times when things were grim and also when they were going especially well—for it's just as important not to lose your head with joy either, especially in a business where the graph of your career resembles a roller coaster. Through all my ups and downs, I have thought of old Frank Goodall and remembered that the happiest man I ever knew was a man for whom sometimes the fish were biting and sometimes not.

Letter to a Little Girl

B Y

F. SCOTT FITZGERALD

EDITOR'S NOTE: *For all of his preoccupation with the jazz age in which he lived, F. Scott Fitzgerald was a devoted father. His daughter—and only child—Frances was one of his main concerns throughout his otherwise unconventional life. She is now the wife of a Washington lawyer and mother of four children. In 1933, when she was 11 years old, and away at camp, Fitzgerald wrote a letter to her which ended with the following wonderful, whimsical advice.*

The letter (copyright 1945 by New Directions) is reprinted in a new book of letters, *The Father,* Evan Jones, editor, published in March 1960 by Rinehart and Company. Dated 1933, this Fitzgerald father-daughter advice is delightful reading any time, but especially on Father's Day!

DEAR PIE:

- *Things to worry about:*

  Worry about courage
  Worry about cleanliness
  Worry about efficiency
  Worry about horsemanship. . . .

- *Things not to worry about:*

  Don't worry about popular opinion
  Don't worry about dolls
  Don't worry about the past
  Don't worry about the future
  Don't worry about growing up

Don't worry about anybody getting ahead of you
Don't worry about triumph
Don't worry about failure unless it comes through your own fault
Don't worry about mosquitoes
Don't worry about flies
Don't worry about insects in general
Don't worry about parents
Don't worry about boys
Don't worry about disappointments
Don't worry about pleasures
Don't worry about satisfactions

- *Things to think about:*

What am I really aiming at?

SCOTT

On Seeing Things Clearly

BY

EMILY KIMBROUGH

NOTED TRAVELER, LECTURER, WRITER

---

*"Nonsense! That would never be noticed
from a trotting horse."*
—MY GRANDMOTHER

A few weeks ago, as I was mounting the steps to a lecture platform, my stocking caught on a sharp edge and was very nearly disintegrated by a run. I paused dismayed, but at that instant's pause a phrase of my grandmother's came back to me.

When a small thing upset someone my grandmother used to say, "Nonsense! That would never be noticed from a trotting horse."

This pronouncement was first directed at me when I was ten. I was complaining bitterly of some defect in my appearance which I thought was bound to draw the attention of every guest at the party for which I was being made ready. Grandmother's image of a trotting horse was impressive to a little girl. I had to admit that a horseman riding by would not notice my shortcoming.

I think I began then to sort out the things that are important from the unimportant.

Through the years, I have conjured up often that ghostly rider. He has become for me an unfailing authority for my own scale of values —important vs. trivial. Have I said or done something unkind, or was it only harmlessly awkward? Have I evaded those things that I ought to have done, or were they not worth doing in the first place? Conversely, have I bridled at an evidence of malice on someone else's part, or was I making something of nothing at all?

In my mind I sometimes cause the rider of the trotting horse to dismount and allow me to take his place. I have found that the back of a trotting horse is also a good site from which to set in proper scale one's personal landscape. It is surprising how many petty annoyances disappear entirely when one rides by them on a trotting horse.

LIVING
WITH
THE
WORLD

Mileposts

B Y

DALE CARNEGIE

AUTHOR OF ''HOW TO STOP WORRYING
AND START LIVING''

*"Anyone can carry his burden, however hard, until nightfall.
Anyone can do his work, however hard, for one day."*
—ROBERT LOUIS STEVENSON

One of the most appalling comments on our present way of life is that half of all our hospital beds are occupied by patients with nervous and mental troubles. And a principal cause is that too many people allow themselves to collapse under the crushing burdens of accumulated yesterdays and fearful tomorrows.

Here is the problem: You and I are standing in this split second at the meeting place of two eternities—the vast past that has endured forever and the future that is plunging on to the last syllable of recorded time. We can't possibly live in either of these eternities, but we often try to do so; and, in the process, we wreck both our bodies and our minds.

The answer, as Stevenson says, is to live for today. Of course, it may be that part of today's work calls for reviewing the past, or planning for tomorrow. But there's no excuse for doing so with panic or regret. Instead we should get the facts and push on from there.

Today is the only time we can possibly live. Let's not turn it into a physical and mental hell by aimless worry about the future. Let's also stop fretting over the blunders we made yesterday.

Remember how a walking trip always seems shorter if we concentrate, not on the total distance to our destination, but just the distance to the next milepost. In the same way, we should concentrate on living within today. Then better tomorrows will inevitably follow.

On Crises

BY

JOHN ERSKINE

AUTHOR AND EDUCATOR

"This time, like all other times, is a very good one, if we but know what to do with it."
—EMERSON

Ralph Waldo Emerson spoke these words in 1837, when most of his hearers at the Harvard Phi Beta Kappa meeting were fed up with Andrew Jackson. That un-Harvard-like person was at the end of his second term, having, as his critics felt, all but wrecked American society and the foundations of national credit. In the circumstances, Emerson went pretty far. He said that the best moment to be born is always during a revolution; that life is just one revolution after another, a series of crises in which we take farewell of the past, and, if we are wise, meet the future. Every time is a good time to live in, if we know what to do with it.

The Art of Success

BY

WILFERD A. PETERSON

AUTHOR OF "THE ART OF LIVING"

"Do not pray for tasks equal to your powers.
Pray for powers equal to your tasks."
—PHILLIPS BROOKS

There are no secrets of success. Success is doing the things you know you should do. Success is not doing the things you know you should not do.

Success is not limited to any one area of your life. It encompasses all of the facets of your relationships: as parent, as wife or husband, as citizen, neighbor, worker and all of the others.

Success is not confined to any one part of your personality but is related to the development of all the parts: body, mind, heart and spirit. It is making the most of your total self.

Success is discovering your best talents, skills and abilities and applying them where they will make the most effective contribution to your fellow men.

Success is focusing the full power of all you are on what you have a burning desire to achieve.

Success is ninety-nine percent mental attitude. It calls for love, joy, optimism, confidence, serenity, poise, faith, courage, cheerfulness, imagination, initiative, tolerance, honesty, humility, patience and enthusiasm.

Success is not arriving at the summit of a mountain as a final destination. It is a continuing upward spiral of progress. It is perpetual growth.

Success is having the courage to meet failure without being defeated. It is refusing to let present loss interfere with your long-range goal.

Success is accepting the challenge of the difficult. In the inspiring words of Phillips Brooks: "Do not pray for tasks equal to your powers. Pray for powers equal to your tasks. Then the doing of your work shall be no miracle, but you shall be the miracle."

Formulas for Fame

B Y

THOMAS A. EDISON

INVENTOR AND GREAT AMERICAN

EDITOR'S NOTE: *In 1961, 30 years after his death, Thomas Alva Edison took his place in the celebrated Hall of Fame at New York University. Below are some "Words to Live By" from this distinctively American genius:*

There is far more opportunity than there is ability.

Education isn't play—and it can't be made to look like play. It is hard, hard work. But it can be made interesting work.

The stomach is the only part of man which can be fully satisfied. The yearning of man's brain for new knowledge and experience and for more pleasant and comfortable surroundings never can be completely met. It is an appetite which cannot be appeased.

We shall have no better conditions in the future if we are satisfied with all those which we have at present.

Everything comes to him who hustles while he waits.

The very first thing an executive must have is a fine memory. Of course it does not follow that a man with a fine memory is necessarily a fine executive. But if he has the memory he has the first qualification, and if he has not the memory nothing else matters.

Restlessness is discontent and discontent is the first necessity of progress. Show me a thoroughly satisfied man—I will show you a failure.

Genius is 1 percent inspiration and 99 percent perspiration.

The best thinking has been done in solitude. The worst has been done in turmoil.

My Magic Bookmark

BY

ALICIA MARKOVA

FAMOUS DANCER

"Let nothing disturb thee;
Let nothing dismay thee:
All things pass;
God never changes.

Patience attains
All that it strives for.
He who has God
Finds he lacks nothing:
God alone suffices."
—ST. TERESA OF AVILA

St. Teresa's Bookmark travels with me everywhere. In a picture frame, it has journeyed around the world with me. Wherever I am, I take it out and set it on my dressing table. And whenever things seem to be going badly, I find comfort in it.

The Bookmark was sent to me when my world seemed to be falling apart. In 1943 I was struck with illness so severe that for the first time in all my long career I was unable to dance. It was frightening. Strength is essential to a ballerina not only in moments of flashing leaps and turns but also for the quiet, controlled movements that give the illusion of being light as thistledown.

I thought—and my thoughts were charged with terror—that I would never again be able to perform in the great and difficult classical ballets to which I had devoted my life.

Then the Bookmark arrived. I read it again and again. Every line offered solace but for me that one line "All things pass" gave me the most comfort and hope. It gave me the patience essential to my recovery. Slowly, I began to realize that pain would pass, and healing come.

Finally, I knew that the message of the Bookmark spoke to me of things other than illness. It spoke to me of a new attitude of mind, an attitude by no means negative. For with patience and fortitude, trouble would pass, releasing energy for positive thought and action.

The months dragged by and at last I was fully recovered. Once more—after a cautious start—I could dance the most exacting roles. And the pain, the heartbreak, the desperation had gone, too, for "All things pass." I was home again; I was living again; I had been reborn.

On Eternity

BY

GEORGE AND HELEN PAPASHVILY

AUTHORS OF "ANYTHING CAN HAPPEN"

"This minute, too, is part of eternity."

When George was a little boy in the Caucasus he was taken once to visit a revered old man who lived all alone, high on a mountain top.

It was customary for each child in the district to give the hermit a gift and receive in return a special proverb or word of advice that he might use as a talisman thereafter through his future life.

The old man had a stern face and a long white beard. He beckoned the boy to come closer. George was frightened but he went. The old man waved the grown people away and then grew friendly. He asked the little boy at his side what he wanted to do and where he wanted to go when he was grown. He told him tales of his own life and his travels over the earth.

After a little while he said, "Now to give you your proverb. I want it to be something that will be of use to you when you are young and when you are old—something to help when you feel sad or tired or discouraged—something to remember when you doubt and fear."

George waited.

The old man bent down and whispered in his ear, "This minute, too, is part of eternity."

George didn't understand it (perhaps he wasn't meant to) until he grew up. For like many simple truths it needs thought and reflection and experience to make it clear.

But once comprehended it affords a whole new perspective of life with vistas as wide as space and as long as time. The simplest act acquires dignity and import; the most fleeting moment, meaning. Birth and death, instead of being two irreconcilable parts, form a harmonious whole.

The Awakening

BY

BORIS PASTERNAK

FAMOUS SOVIET WRITER,
AUTHOR OF "DOCTOR ZHIVAGO"

---

*"The wise man looks inside his heart
and finds eternal peace."*
—HINDU PROVERB

In this era of world wars, in this atomic age, the values have changed. We have learned that we are the guests of existence, travelers between two stations. We must discover security within ourselves.

During our short span of life we must find our own insights into our relationship with the existence in which we participate so briefly. Otherwise, we cannot live. This means, as I see it, a departure from the materialistic view of the nineteenth century. It means a reawakening of the spiritual world, of our inner life—of religion. I don't mean religion as a dogma or as a church, but as a vital feeling.

God's Open Door

BY

DR. A. J. CRONIN

AUTHOR OF "THE CITADEL" AND
"A THING OF BEAUTY"

"If God shuts one door, He opens another."
—IRISH PROVERB

Thirty years ago, when I was a doctor in London, on the point of moving to a specialist's practice in Harley Street, my health broke down. I was told that I must take a year's rest and that, even so, I might never again be fit to stand the wear and tear of medical life.

What a blow! I liked my work. From the humblest beginnings in a small Welsh mining practice, I had slaved to achieve this objective. And now, on the threshold of success, the door was slammed in my face. My state of mind was such that I could not help voicing bitterness and resentment to my friends.

One of these was an old Irish nun, the Reverend Mother of the Bon Secours, a small order of nursing sisters who occupied a house quite near mine in Westbourne Grove, and who frequently looked after my patients. She heard my outburst in silence, then said:

"You know, Doctor, we have a saying in Ireland, that if God shuts one door, He opens another."

I did not give her remark a second thought and soon after left for my place of exile, a remote district in the West Highlands. Here time hung heavy upon my hands. Suddenly, out of the blue, I had an impulse to write. I began a novel, *Hatter's Castle,* and I finished it, packed it up, and sent it to a publisher who accepted it! Out of all reason, a door had opened. A new career lay before me.

So many of us, meeting with sudden disappointment, misfortune or defeat, raise a cry of anger and resentment against heaven. Why should God do this to us? To be deprived of health, miss the chance of promotion, to lose one's job, these things are hard to bear, and harder perhaps to understand.

Yet we cannot measure Divine Providence by the yardstick of human mentality. What we think an evil may well be for eventual good.

The demands life makes may seem hard at times, yet we ought not to whine. God never takes without giving something in return. Disappointments and troubles are often the instruments with which He fashions us for better things to come.

Life is no straight and easy corridor along which we travel free and unhampered, but a maze of passages, through which we must seek our way, now lost and confused, now checked in a blind alley. But always, if we have faith, God will open a door for us, not perhaps one that we ourselves would ever have thought of, but one that will ultimately prove good for us.

A General Looks at God

BY

MAJOR GENERAL JOHN B. MEDARIS, U. S. A. (RET.)

FORMER COMMANDING GENERAL,
U.S. ARMY ORDNANCE MISSILE COMMAND

"The Universe is centered on neither the Earth
nor the Sun—it is centered on God."
—ALFRED NOYES

In this busy age, in these days of intense scientific activity as we approach the conquest of space, it is not surprising that we find ourselves restless, unfulfilled, unsatisfied.

Amidst all this kaleidoscopic movement the inner soul of man must find an eternal harbor, some home port that will stay put, his own internal haven of peace. When he fails to find such an anchorage his mind refuses the challenge of change. Mental illness becomes an epidemic of the times.

And youth, cast afloat on uncharted seas, lacks assurance. The cry of pain and insecurity rises from the hearts of the untrained—"Where am I?" . . . "Where am I going?" . . . "Who and where is the authority?" And the world is too busy to answer.

Yet the answer is there, the answer without which man becomes a scurrying animal without purpose or direction, fighting for the next morsel of food.

The answer is in the majestic order of the universe and its obedience to unchanging law.

The answer is there—in the certainty and regularity of the seasons, in the march of the sun, the moon, and the stars, in the regular coming of night and day, in the balance between man's consumption of life-giving oxygen and its production by the plant life of the earth, in the regularity of change from the barren silence of winter to the greening, growing life of spring, in the cry of a newborn child with its ever-new demonstration of the miracle of life.

This timeless, changeless order is an assurance of unchallenged authority, a sign of safe anchorage for the troubled spirit of man.

Increase in man's knowledge does not mean the discovery of new things, but only the extension of his understanding and ability to use that which already is, and has always been. Like the growth of a child from infant to adult, man is "discovering" worlds new to him—but old to God.

When this is fully realized, man can stand straight and tall, assured in the face of apparent uncertainty, secure in his knowledge of the way home, at peace with himself because he is at peace with Almighty God.

The Ultimate Victory

B Y

DR. THOMAS A. DOOLEY

EDITOR'S NOTE: *The late Dr. Dooley, known to thousands of his native patients in Laos as "Dr. Tom," was a great medical missionary, builder of hospitals, humanitarian. He was also a man of profound religious faith. One of his last letters, written from a hospital in Hong Kong to Father Theodore Hesburgh, president of Notre Dame University, contains this unforgettable passage:*

When the time comes, like now, then the storm around me does not matter. Nothing human or earthly can touch me. A wilder storm of peace gathers in my heart. What seems unpossessable, I can possess. . . . What is unutterable, I can utter. Because I can pray, I can communicate. How do people endure anything on earth if they cannot have God?

The Common Bond

BY

SAMUEL HOPKINS ADAMS

NOVELIST AND BIOGRAPHER

"I am a man; nothing that concerns mankind is alien to me."
—TERENCE

This saying, for me, is touched with fire. It is as significant today as when its author wrote it in Rome twenty-one centuries ago.

It has a strange origin, that pronouncement of Terence. Born a slave and raised to a class and a nationality whose imperial boast was, "I am a Roman; the world belongs to me," the youthful comedian was the first to affirm the principle of a common kinship. His message came down the ages. Jesus Christ preached it. Milton and Walt Whitman caught and carried on its spirit. Thomas Paine paraphrased it. Pope and Tennyson turned it into living verse. No man ever bettered its utterance.

Never before has the message of solidarity been so gravely needed. We are living at a time when creeds and ideologies vary and clash. But the gospel of human sympathy is universal and eternal.

"Who's Next?"

BY

JOHN R. TUNIS

SPORTSWRITER-TURNED-AUTHOR

The shirt-sleeved man standing beside the barber chair flipped the apron twice and turned to the three customers sitting by the wall. Again he called out:

"Who's next?"

One of the men put down his paper, rose, took off his coat, hung it on the wall and slipped into the chair. The other two paid no attention. They went on reading.

Just as simple as that. The governor, the bank president, the workman are all equal in the eyes of the law and the barber. Yet this scene that takes place every day in every village, town, and city in the United States is the essence of democracy . . . of respect for the rights of other men . . . of co-operation . . . of decency and fair play.

Listen to the two men who are waiting. One is reading the sports pages. After a while he puts the paper down.

"Looks like the Cards will breeze in."

"You mean the Dodgers."

"The Dodgers! You're crazy. The Cards are the team with the pitchers."

"Well, okay. You're entitled to your opinion. This is a free country."

"Who's next?" . . . "This is a free country." . . . You have heard the words a thousand times. So have I. So has every person in this country. Heard them without thinking. Without realizing that this scene and these phrases that we take for granted are part of the deep concepts of a democratic nation. You would never hear them said in lands ruled by totalitarian leaders. There the boss is always right; he can't be questioned. Nor would you hear many other statements we use in our daily life:

"First come, first served."

"He's got his rights."

"May the best man win."

"Give him a break."

"Fair and square."

These expressions are verbal symbols. They mean something to every American. In fact they register to every human being no matter where he lives. They are the everyday Words to Live By of a democracy.

The Uncommon Man

BY

HERBERT HOOVER

FORMER PRESIDENT OF THE UNITED STATES

*"That nation is proudest and noblest and most exalted which
has the greatest number of really great men."*
—SINCLAIR LEWIS

Recently, in my opinion, there has been too much talk about the Common Man. It has been dinned into us that this is the Century of the Common Man. The idea seems to be that the Common Man has come into his own at last.

Thus we are in danger of developing a cult of the Common Man, which means a cult of mediocrity. But there is at least one hopeful sign: I have never been able to find out who this Common Man is. In fact, most Americans, and especially women, will get mad and fight if you try calling them common.

This is hopeful because it shows that most people are holding fast to an essential fact in American life. We believe in equal opportunity for all, but we know that this includes the opportunity to rise to leadership—in other words, to be uncommon.

Let us remember that the great human advances have not been brought about by mediocre men and women. They were brought about by distinctly uncommon people with vital sparks of leadership. Many of the great leaders were, it is true, of humble origin, but that alone was not their greatness.

It is a curious fact that when you get sick you want an uncommon doctor; if your car breaks down you want an uncommonly good mechanic; when we get into war we want dreadfully an uncommon admiral and an uncommon general.

I have never met a father and mother who did not want their children to grow up to be uncommon men and women. May it always be so. For the future of America rests not in mediocrity, but in the constant renewal of leadership in every phase of our national life.

77

The Rent We Pay

BY

LORD HALIFAX

FORMER BRITISH AMBASSADOR TO THE U. S.

"Service is the rent we pay for our room on earth."

These are words which, if I remember them correctly, are used at the meetings of "Toc H," a society organized by British servicemen in the Ypres salient during the First World War. From the first time I heard them, they made a profound impression on me.

We have been too much inclined to let our thoughts rest upon what we judge to be our rights, without giving equal weight to the recognition of our duties. But in these words the balance is set right, and the claim is made on every one of us to serve our fellows.

There is no room in the modern world for easy indifference to the world's needs: we are all our "brother's keeper." Only by translating this truth into terms of daily life can we hope to establish true understanding between men and nations—and make the world more worthy of all the sacrifice that twice in a generation has been spent to save it.

Beauty

BY

FRANK LLOYD WRIGHT

ARCHITECT

" 'Beauty is truth, truth beauty,'—that is all ye know on
earth and all ye need to know."
—JOHN KEATS

People are forever saying, "Oh, that's beautiful but it isn't practical." As an architect more than sixty years, I have learned that only the beautiful is practical. And conversely, anything that is truly practical, functional and useful is beautiful—whether it be a sunset or some man-made object. When we perceive a thing to be beautiful, it is because we instinctively recognize its rightness.

You can apply "the practical is beautiful" or "the beautiful is practical" principle to your everyday life, whether you live in a castle or a hut. The beautiful is not ornate or needlessly expensive. On the contrary, excess is always vulgar.

But you must first learn to recognize the beautiful, have the disposition to cherish it and the intelligence to distinguish it from what is merely curious. When we lack the knowledge of the difference, we find ugliness—never beauty. Today, unfortunately, many human beings, like bushels of grain, are poured out and trampled in our cities. But the eventual City of the Future will contain all of the practical products of industry and yet have beauty for every inhabitant.

In everyday life, you can be guided by beauty in whatever you undertake—whether making a dress or a bookcase. To achieve the superior, you must first refuse to accept the inferior. Look for the light and you won't dwell in darkness. You will then bring out something in yourself which is both practical and beautiful.

The longer I live the more beautiful life becomes. The earth's beauty grows on me. If you foolishly ignore beauty, you'll soon find yourself without it. Your life will be impoverished. But if you wisely invest in beauty, it will remain with you all the days of your life.

I Say What I Think

BY

LILLI PALMER

STAGE AND SCREEN STAR

"Everybody's friend is everybody's fool."
—MY MOTHER

My mother was born on the river Rhine, where people are gay and easygoing, where they drink much wine and don't care who likes them. When I was a child I often heard from her a healthy warning, especially when I came crying that someone didn't like me and demanding to know what I could do to make him or her like me.

"Everybody's friend is everybody's fool," she would say serenely; or sometimes, "Many enemies mean much honor," or "Where there's much sun there's much shadow."

I have interpreted those ideas in my own way. I don't set out to antagonize people, or to be aggressive or provocative, but I have never made a special concession just for the purpose of being liked. I've spoken my mind even when I knew that what I said might be un-popular, because I believe that to speak your mind is essential, to take part in a controversy is important. It has never been my nature to sit back and keep quiet for fear of treading on somebody's toes.

The danger of being too sensitive to what others think is strongly illustrated in the play *Death of a Salesman*. The author makes an important cause of the demoralization of his hero the fact that he cared too much whether he was well liked. He was afraid ever to make an enemy, and this hastened his destruction.

My mother made me immune to that fear in early youth. You can't go through life only making friends, I realized very soon.

If, for a good cause, you must make an enemy, accept the fact. As long as your conscience is clear, you will find that you have strengthened not only your determination but your character.

One Thing at a Time

BY

EDDIE ALBERT

MOTION PICTURE ACTOR AND PRODUCER

"Appreciate the moment."
—ISAMU NOGUCHI

I met Isamu Noguchi, the American-born Japanese sculptor and designer, when I went to Japan in 1956 to make *The Teahouse of the August Moon*. At a time of tension, he gave me some advice which changed my whole life. In honesty, I use and enjoy it today with every breath I take.

The monsoon had caught us, darkening the skies with rain, holding up our picture six weeks. We were fatigued and depressed. I had seen little of the charm and beauty of Japan so, before we left, I asked Noguchi if he would show me something he considered lovely, and characteristic, maybe a Zen Buddhist Temple.

I expected this famous artist to reveal a sight special and exotic, something to marvel at. I was disappointed when he took me out in the country from Nara, a small town near Kyoto, and pointed to an old farmhouse. We entered a large bare room. There was no altar and no priest, no Oriental mystery. An incredibly old woman served us tea. I crouched on the hard floor, my knees hurting, as she brought one thing at a time—a bowl, a copper pot, a tray and so on. We went through the traditional formal ceremonies.

"Now shall we appreciate the utensils?" Noguchi asked. An odd remark! But he went on: "The ceremony was to slow you down with one thing at a time. What you must learn is to appreciate the moment."

He picked up a bowl that had been in front of me for half an hour. I had not really looked at it. Now, as Noguchi turned it in his hands, I saw it for the first time. It was delightfully curved, glowing with a rich gold patina. Then Noguchi motioned toward a slim vase containing three delicate flowers, artfully arranged. I had taken them for granted.

"One thing at a time," Noguchi repeated gently. "Appreciate the moment."

My depression vanished. Ever since then, I have found life exhilarating wherever I am, even in times of stress.

It was strange that an American like me had to go to Japan to learn how to live. But I think I appreciate that moment with Noguchi more than any other in my life—except, of course, this wonderful moment of being alive and knowing it *right now*.

The Arch

BY

IRWIN EDMAN

PHILOSOPHER AND AUTHOR OF
''PHILOSOPHER'S QUEST''

"Yet all experience is an arch wherethro'
Gleams that untravell'd world whose margin fades
For ever and for ever when I move."
—TENNYSON

When I was very young I thought that some day I should arrive at a fixed and final version of the truth, lighting upon it in the pages of a book or in some sudden bright new page of life. But as one grows older the force of Tennyson's words grows stronger. Before one lies an untraveled realm and a constantly changing one. The world appears different at fifty than it did at twenty, or one has learned nothing. And if the world looks different to the same mind at two periods of a man's life, by the same token it looks and must look different to different persons even in the same era.

In this book a group of contemporaries have made comments on quotations that have been for each of them Words to Live By. Each man, of course, must ultimately live by his own words in his own way and see nature and man through his own arch of experience. But it is the same world we all live in, and essentially the same human nature we share. That is why communication is possible and why we can learn from each other's experience. A philosophy is inevitably the result of one man's temperament and history. But any man's world-view becomes more generous and imaginative and liberated when he succeeds, if only for the time being, in seeing through the eyes of others and vicariously sharing their quest.